ANTHOLOGY OF INSTRUMENTAL MUSIC
FROM THE END OF THE SIXTEENTH
TO THE
END OF THE SEVENTEENTH CENTURY

Da Capo Press Music Reprint Series

ANTHOLOGY OF INSTRUMENTAL MUSIC
FROM THE END OF THE SIXTEENTH
TO THE
END OF THE SEVENTEENTH CENTURY

[Instrumentalsätze vom Ende des XVI. bis Ende des XVII. Jahrhunderts]

Compiled and edited by Joseph Wilhelm von Wasielewski

New Introduction and Notes by John G. Suess,
Case Western Reserve University

DA CAPO PRESS • NEW YORK • 1974

Library of Congress Cataloging in Publication Data

Wasielewski, Wilhelm Joseph von, 1822-1896, comp.
    Anthology of instrumental music from the end of
the sixteenth to the end of the seventeenth century.

    (Da Capo Press music reprint series)
    Originally issued in 1874 as the music suppl. to
Wasielewski's Die Violine im XVII. Jahrhundert und
die Anfänge der Instrumentalcomposition.
    Bibliography: p.
    1. Instrumental music—To 1800. 2. Chamber music
—To 1800. 3. Music, Italian. I. Wasielewski,
Wilhelm Joseph von, 1882-1896. Die Violine im XVII.
Jahrundert und die Anfänge der Instrumental composition.
II. Title.
M2.W225   785.7'1   68-14325
ISBN 0-306-70951-1

This Da Capo press edition of
Anthology of Instrumental Music from the End of the Sixteenth to the End of the Seventeenth Century
is an unabridged republication of
Instrumentalsätze vom Ende des XVI. bis Ende des XVII. Jahrhunderts,
published originally in Bonn in 1874.
It includes as well the table of contents and composer index added to the Berlin reissue (*c.* 1900),
and a new introduction and notes by John G. Suess.

INTRODUCTION

Joseph Wilhelm von Wasielewski (1822–1896) was a violinist and composer as well as an author, but it is primarily his writings that have given him a significant place in musicology. He studied with Mendelssohn, David, and Hauptman at the Leipzig Conservatory, and was a personal friend of Schumann. Wasielewski conducted orchestras in Bonn, Düsseldorf, and Dresden and also was a music critic to the *Leipziger Zeitung,* the *Dresdener Journal,* and other publications. Despite his multiple contributions to various periodicals, his importance as a scholar lies in two other major areas of publication: biography and history. His biographical works on Beethoven (1888), Schumann (1858), and Karl Reinecke (1892) are important contributions to the field of musicology, but it was in his historical publications that Wasielewski created landmarks in previously uncharted areas of musical scholarship. His interest in scholarship combined with his love for string instruments resulted in such classics as *Die Violine und ihre Meister* (Bonn: M. Cohen, 1869); *Die Violine im XVII Jahrhundert und die Anfänge der Instrumental composition* (Bonn: M. Cohen, 1874), and its companion volume of musical examples, *Instrumentalsätze vom Ende des XVI bis Ende des XVII Jahrhunderts* (Bonn: M. Cohen, 1874); *Geschichte der Instrumentalmusik im XVI Jahrhundert* (Berlin: Guttenberg, 1878); and *Das Violoncell und seine Geschichte* (Leipzig: Breitkopf & Härtel, 1889). Several editions were published of each of these works.

The *Instrumentalsätze vom Ende des XVI bis Ende des XVII Jahrhunderts* is a collection of music which Wasielewski compiled mainly from the conservatory library in Bologna and the state libraries of Brussels and Berlin. This monumental collection is devoted almost totally to the illustration of the evolution of Italian instrumental ensemble music in the seventeenth century, with no concern for keyboard or lute music, and only a few examples of solo string works. Because of the specific emphasis of this collection on seventeenth century instrumental ensemble music, it seems appropriate and indeed necessary to provide a brief resumé of some of the more significant developments in this area of musical composition. Despite the usual pitfalls of overgeneralization and oversimplification, it is hoped that this discussion, which has been deliberately limited to the *canzona* and sonata, will help to provide a frame of reference for Wasielewski's fine collection.

The major categories of late sixteenth-century instrumental music in Italy include dances, variations, the *ricercar,* the fantasy, and the *canzona.* Paired dances (in duple plus triple meter) and many-variation schemes were generally written for keyboard instruments or lute. The same may be said for the polyphonically constructed *ricercar* and the fantasy, between which, at this time, there was little differentiation except in name. On the other hand, the *canzona,* or *canzona per sonar* became a major vehicle for the development of instrumental ensemble music. While the motet was the prototype for the polyphonically strict *ricercar,* the *chanson* was the model for the *canzona.* By its nature and tradition the chanson provided a basis for a less consistent polyphonic texture as well as contrasting sections, yet it does not appear to have ever been as totally dominated by textual considerations as either the motet or madrigal. It, therefore, allowed the composer to concentrate more on problems of musical logic. Since the composer of instrumental music had no text to use for the foundation of the musical form, he became concerned with principles of musical organization intrinsic to the music itself. The *canzona* was apparently the most suitable category for experimentation with the formal organization of musical materials.

By 1600, the *canzona* had achieved a number of general characteristics which tended to identify it: it was generally for similar instruments (a consort of four to six); the melodic materials still reflected the vocal tendencies of the *chanson* in smallness of range and in the employment of dactylic rhythmic motives; the Flemish polyphonic texture was also strongly implied with much use of imitative entries and short canons; unlike the madrigal tradition, the *canzona* was written with a rather conservative conception of harmony and tonality, and little chromaticism is found in it; the *canzona* is modal, with a strong emphasis on the dorian, ionian, and mixolydian modes; and the formal conceptions for ordering the musical materials emphasize repetition and/or recapitulation, variation, and contrast in a multisectional framework.

These concepts are immediately recognizable in the works by Maschera and Gabrieli printed in this collection. The general search for abstract musical ideas as a means for controlling musical materials is reflected in the work of these two composers, and particularly in Giovanni Gabrieli. His *canzoni* and *sonate* (meaning only a sounded or played piece at this time) reveal his concern for acoustical problems closely associated with antiphonal practices and multiple directionality of sound as well as with abstract formal organization. Gabrieli's attention to the combination and contrasts of sonorities resulted in texture which moved away from polyphony and turned instead toward chordal sections and clear indications of tonal harmony; yet, this was still done within the multisectional *canzona* framework and the abstract unifying musical conceptions of repetition, variation, and recapitulation. This innovation, along with his development of dynamic contrasts and dialogue technique mark Gabrieli as a major contributor to the evolution of instrumental music.

The Arrival of the Baroque Sonata (ca. 1600-1650)

One of the most difficult problems associated with the arrival of Baroque instrumental music in the early seventeenth century is one of a meaningful nomenclature capable of delimiting the various musical categories. Since the first half of the seventeenth century was one of change and transition, the categories of instrumental music were also in a state of flux, and only the improvisational types, such as the capriccio and toccata, generally maintained their flexible meaning.

Collections of dances for every conceivable grouping of instruments, solo and ensemble, became very popular during the first half of the seventeenth century. They are sometimes found grouped by type, which allowed the performers to match them, or in an order of thematically linked coupled dances—generally, a paired duple and triple rhythm dance. In most cases, the style reflects a rather homophonic approach (see No. 9), with a bipartite structure incorporating repeat signs. Pairs or groups of dances are found in the same collections of music that include sonatas. As early as 1607, Salamone Rossi applied the trio instrumentation to *balletti* and *gagliardes,* and the binary sectional dance soon became an accepted chamber work. Already, in his *Arie madrigali et corenti* (1620), Biagio Marini includes incipient dance suites, and gradually these "suites" absorbed the standard Baroque dances, such as the *corrente* and *courant, sarabanda, giga, brando,* and others. Virtually all composers of instrumental ensemble music at this time wrote dances as well as sonatas, canzonas, and other types of music.

The variation also became an important part of the musical literature for instrumental ensembles. Most prominent in these instrumental variations was the use of *ostinato* basses or simply bass patterns. The renaissance dance melodies that particularly emphasized patterns of functional harmony (I, IV, V) were used either as an *ostinato* pattern or as the basis for the harmony on the first beat of each measure (see No. 10). Some of the common patterns were the *passamezzo (antico* and *moderno),* the *folia,* the *romanesca,* the *ruggiero,* and the *ciaconna* or *passacaglia,* but many others were also used. These variations were generally sectional, often called *partita,* with fixed patterns of figuration for each section.

The *canzona* was still one of the most significant categories for instrumental ensemble music in the early seventeenth century, but it soon became confused, and was identified with the term "sonata" until the middle of the century. This confusion in terminology leads to the realization that both the *canzona* and the new Baroque sonata were flexible terms at this time, allowing composers to create a great variety of solutions before the sonata was clearly codified. The conservative *canzona* in the 1620's generally consisted of four equal voices, with the bass voice taking on more and more of a bass function; an extensive polyphonic texture and many imitative entries; a multisectional structure including short homophonic insertions; subjects based on dactylic rhythms; and simple repetition, variation, and recapitulation schemes for unity. The progressive *canzona*—usually with fewer than four voices—and the sonata are sufficiently similar in style that they may be treated together.

The ensemble sonata, or basically the trio sonata, was born in northern Italy in the early seventeenth century, and its creation seems largely to have been the result of the influence of monody upon pre-existing instrumental music. The rise of the polarity of melody and bass, along with the stabilization of the *basso continuo,* provided an enormous impetus to the development of the solo and trio sonata. The solo sonata has a direct link to vocal tradition through the instrumentally accompanied solo song and monody, while the trio sonata, in particular, and the ensemble sonata, in general, appear to have a close relation to dialogue and *concertato* concepts. The trio texture is one of the major stylistic characteristics associated with the rise of seventeenth century instrumental ensemble music. Despite the need for further study, several scholars have provided reasonable explanations for the evolution of the trio texture, which appears to have both vocal and instrumental sources in the madrigal, *canzonetta,* and *chanson,* as well as in the *canzona* and *ricercar.*[1] The multi-voiced madrigal, motet and *canzonetta* could have absorbed the middle parts in the melody lines and *basso continuo,* as is apparent in Monteverdi's *Scherzi musicali* (1607), where vocal duets over a *basso continuo* alternate with instrumental *ritornelli* of similar texture. The trio texture could also have been derived through the multi-voiced instrumental *canzona, ricercar,* or *fantasia,* where the middle parts could simply have become less significant. This occurs mainly when the soprano and bass parts provide the illusion of more parts by employing multiple statements of the subject at the points of imitation, causing the middle parts to lose their melodic function and to become more closely associated with the *basso continuo.* Finally, the trio texture may have evolved through the addition of a second part to monody. In some of the madrigal collections of Salamone Rossi (1602, 1603), all the parts but the soprano voice have *basso continuo* indicated as a possible substitute. In 1607, Rossi wrote the first instrumental trio, and in his last two collections of instrumental music (1622, 1623), he limits himself exclusively to trio settings. In any case, the basic reduction of the four to six-voice texture to the trio texture, and its emergence as primary texture type, even in instrumental compositions with more than three voices, is one of the significant changes in instrumental music of the early seventeenth century.

The trio *canzona* or sonata is a category of Baroque instrumental ensemble music whose forces generally consist of two melody lines of equal importance, balanced by a *basso continuo* for harmonic support. The two titles that most commonly refer to this category are *canzona* (or *sonata) a due* and *canzona* (or *sonata) a tre.* The two titles differ mainly in that the bass instrument which supports the *basso continuo* line simply doubles the bass line in the *a due,* while it has a more independent function in the *a tre.* The ensemble may result in a texture of up to four parts in the *a due,* and up to five parts in the *a tre,* if one includes the improvised realization of the basso continuo. It is rare, however, to have a contrapuntal texture of more than three voices, except for multiple imitative entries that may create the illusion of a larger number of parts. In Baroque instrumental music, the trio texture is then a synthesis of the *stile concertato,* with its separation of function between melodic and harmonic lines clearly delineated, and the *stile concertante,* with equal importance given to the melodic lines. In this sense, the trio texture may be considered an ideal compromise between Baroque monody and Renaissance polyphony. In addition, the melodic lines of the trio texture provided a potential for dramatic

dialogue to the same type as that which formed a basis for much of the dramatic vocal music in the opera, oratorio, and cantata.

While the conservative *canzona* tended toward the polyphonic tradition of the Renaissance, the progressive *canzona*-sonata relied upon the new Baroque stylistic directions. Whether solo or multiple voice, the sonata was not a firmly established musical category until after the middle of the seventeenth century.

The rise of the Baroque sonata reveals the evolution of Italian instrumental ensemble and solo music in the seventeenth century. Although Giovanni Gabrieli used the term sonata for his *Sonata pian e forte* (see No. 4), it was not until 1610 that the earliest solo and ensemble sonatas entitled "sonata" were published. Giovanni Paolo Cima's publication, *Concerti ecclesiastici a 1, 2, 3, 4, con sei sonate, per instrumenti a 2, 3, e 4,* demonstrates how sonatas were often included in collections of sacred or secular vocal music, as well as of instrumental chamber music for a variety of instrumentations. As sets of sonatas became independent collections, the number of works in a set was reduced from many, to around six to twelve sonatas per opus, after 1650.

The instrumentation for the ensemble sonata also changed with time. The earliest sonatas frequently had no designation of specific instruments, and they emphasized the equal importance of the *viole* or the *cornetto* and the violin as melody instruments, as in Biagio Marini's *Affetti musicale* [1617]. By the 1630's and 1640's, however, the violin was consistently the most important instrument, until the eighteenth century, when the recorder and transverse flute competed for equality with the violin as melody instruments. In the early sonatas, the *basso continuo* part appears to have been played by a variety of multiple-voice instruments, such as the lute, *tiorba,* and *chitarrone,* as well as keyboard instruments, usually the organ. The harpsichord was specified as early as 1621 (Castello), and soon became particularly popular to the *basso continuo* for dance suites or chamber sonatas. The single-voice bass instruments most commonly used to support the *basso continuo* were the *viola da gamba,* the *violone,* and the violoncello, although the trombone and bassoon were also used.

The earliest Baroque solo and ensemble sonatas (as in the Cima collection of 1610) reveal a close affinity to the *canzona* in having a multisectional form consisting of a number of contrasting short sections differing from each other in rhythm or texture, and generally based on points of imitation, though with-

---

[1] See the studies listed in the Bibliography by Brockhoff, Crocker, Newman, Riemann, Rowan, Schenk, Schering, Schlossberg and Suess.

out the polyphonic emphasis found in the *canzona*. The broad concept of the sonata, however, allowed this musical category to be the center of musical experimentation, and the many different solutions indicate its flexibility in conception and character. These solutions also reflect the ability of the sonata virtually to absorb the characteristics of the various types of instrumental and vocal music contemporary with it.

Some of the primary composers, with publication dates of their collections, in this early period of sonata experimentation are: Negri (1611), Marini (1617, 1629, 1644), Castello (1621, 1629), Fontana (1641), and Neri (1644, 1651) in Venice; S. Rossi (1607, 1608, 1622, 1623) and Buonamente (1626, 1629, 1636, 1637) in Mantua; Turini (1621) in Brescia; Cima (1610) in Milan; Merula (1637, 1651) in Cremona; Cazzati (1642, 1648) in Mantua and Bozzolo; Uccellini (1639, 1642, 1645, 1649) in Modena; Ferro (1649) and Valentini (1621) in Vienna; Farina (1626, 1627, 1628) in Dresden; and Staden (1643) and Kindermann (1640, 1642, 1643, 1653) in Nürnberg.

These composers reflect the relations of early sonata composition to monody, improvisation, variation, program, dance, and the *canzona*. The sonatas of Rossi and Negri reveal the effect of monody with their *ritornello* character, the use of binary and ternary structures, the sparse use of imitation, and the emphasis on homophonic writing in parallel thirds and sixths. In addition, sometimes the bass lines of vocal arias were utilized for instrumental works, as in Rossi's *Sonata decima sopra l'aria della romanesca* (1622).

The improvisational approach, closely linked to vocal performance practices and to the development of idiomatic violin technique, appears in many of the works by composers such as Marini, Castello, Farina, and Uccellini. The virtuosic development of violin technique may be seen in the *concertante* passagework, the expansion to higher positions—up to the sixth position in Uccellini's Opus 5 (1649)—arpeggiated passages, multiple stops, and unusual slurring practices in the sonatas of Castello, Farina, and Uccellini. Special string effects also became popular (see No. 11). The tremolo occurs in Marini's Opus 1, *Affetti musicali* (1617), seven years before Monteverdi's use of the *stile concitato*. In his Opus 8 (1628), Marini also utilizes other affective devices as *groppi, affetti, tardi, scordatura,* and *piano* and *forte* dynamics. In addition, such special effects as *col legno, sul ponticello, pizzicato, vibrato,* and improvised *passagi* also quickly became commonly known to the violinist and composer in the first half of the seventeenth century.

The variation approach in the sonata is clearly exhibited in the popularity of bass patterns such as the *chaconne, romanesca, ruggiero, bergamasca, folia,*

and others, as well as in melodic variation forms. It is common to find variation sonatas mixed in with other types of sonatas and *canzonas* in the instrumental collections by composers such as Buonamente, Turini, Merula, Uccellini, and Marini (see No. 10).

Another favorite sonata type, especially in sonata collections by Farina, Marini, Merula, and Uccellini, is the program sonata with its descriptive titles and musical sound effects. Merula imitates a hen in his "La Gallina" *canzona* (1637), and Farina's *Capriccio stravagante* has musical descriptions of dogs, cats, and other animals, as well as imitations of the sound of other instruments (see No. 11).

The antiphonal *concertato* style associated with the Venetian polychoral tradition also occurs in the early sonata literature. The antiphonal application of the dialogue concept between groups of instruments, each group generally consisting of a separate trio instrumentation, occurs in some of the sonatas of S. Rossi, Buonamente, and Bernardi. They remind one of Gabrieli's *Canzoni per sonar* (see No. 4). In addition, the dialogue concept is inherent in the trio texture, where the two melodic lines generally discuss the same subject material consistently throughout the section.

Fugal composition in the sonata is directly associated with the *canzona,* which became identified with the sonata to such a degree that the terms became virtually synonymous between 1630 and 1660. The three main structures found in these *canzona*-sonatas are the recapitulation form of A B A (A = duple meter movements with points of imitation, and B = triple meter homophonic movements), the variation form with the same basic materials in all movements, and the repetition form where thematic materials are repeated almost identically in all movements. As with the *canzona,* the subjects of the polyphonic movements of the sonata are usually concise short motives which use repeated notes, dactylic rhythms, and have a narrow range. The slow movements are generally homophonic with rhythmic flexibility and expressive melodies. While the bass generally takes part in the polyphony of the ensemble in the *canzona,* the harmonic function is of primary concern in the sonata.

After 1630 the sonata and the *canzona* undergo many changes in their common characteristics: the number of multi-thematic sections in both is reduced to a few (three to six) monothematic movements, which are enlarged; the modal resources in both are reduced to closely allied modes, such as ionic and mixolydian or dorian and aeolian, which are interchanged and alternated when desirable; there is consistent and increasing codification of dissonance usage and its preparation in both the *canzona* and sonata. As both came to utilize the musical elements that tended to separate them, the separation disappeared. Virtuosic writing, for example, had almost disappeared in the ensemble sonata by 1650.

The expansion in the size of the ensemble sonata is reflected by the average length of the sonatas of several composers. Rossi's sonatas from the 1620's average about 55 measures, Uccellini's sonatas of the 1640's average about 90 measures, and Giovanni Legrenzi's sonatas of the 1650's average about 140 measures. This expansion results from the ever-increasing employment of such devices as sequence (harmonic and melodic) and motivic extension (*fortspinnung*) to a goal, namely the cadence. This forward motion required a control device—functional harmony and tonality, the incipient stages of which are particularly clear in the works of composers such as Buonamente, Uccellini, and Cazzati.

The expansion of the ensemble sonata from northern Italy to Austria, Germany, France, and England is well discussed in William S. Newman's *The Sonata in the Baroque Era.* The ensemble sonata rose to prominence in those musical centers of Europe where an established court or church institution provided a demand, and where publishers eagerly desired to meet this demand. Musical centers such as Venice, Bologna, Modena, Rome, Vienna, Salzburg, Munich, Dresden, Leipzig, Berlin, Hamburg, Paris, London, and Amsterdam were focal points of sonata composition and publication. Other reasons for the international expansion of the Italian sonata include the attraction of foreign musicians to famous Italian musical centers for instruction (e.g., Rosenmüller and Händel in Rome and Venice), and the warm welcome received by Italian musicians at the courts of Europe (e.g., Marini, Locatelli, and Geminiani).

The Codification of the Ensemble Sonata
By the middle of the seventeenth century the Italian ensemble sonata had absorbed the characteristics of most other types of instrumental music sufficiently that composers limited themselves mainly to composing collections of sonatas or dances, and the instrumentation was primarily that of the trio sonata. When speaking of the sonata in the last half of the seventeenth century, it is the trio sonata that is the major category of musical composition and performance for instruments. The primary confusion in terms of the instrumental ensemble music of the last half of the seventeenth century is mainly between *sonata* and *sinfonia,* although even *concerto* and *sonata* occasionally are interchangeable.

Of the three main functions of Baroque music—the court, the church, and the theater—the ensemble sonata is primarily associated with the court and the church. It provided entertainment for court functions, and with time it also became diversional chamber music for the middle class. In addition to entertainment, the ensemble sonata also became a favorite medium for musical performance by aristocratic dilletantes.

As a functional work in the church, the ensemble sonata was apparently admitted into the liturgy of the Mass and Vespers, if one accepts the credible thesis that a sonata could replace virtually any organ piece (see A. Banchieri, *L'Organo suonarino,* 1605 and 1611, and G. Frescobaldi, *Fiori musicali,* 1635). A sonata, or portions of it, may have been played before the Mass, before the Kyrie (Introit), in place of the Gradual or Offertory or Communion, to accompany the Elevation, and/or as a postlude. A sonata might be heard before or after Vespers, or in place of antiphons for the Psalms and the Magnificat.

Up to the middle of the seventeenth century, the designation of *Sonata da camera* or *Sonata da chiesa* appears to have had little meaning except that the sonata was acceptable for either function (T. Merula, *Canzoni overo sonate concertate per chiesa, e camera,* 1637). A clear differentiation in character and style based upon function appears after 1650 in B. Marini's *Diversi generi di sonate, da chiesa, e da camera* (1655) and G. Legrenzi's *Suonate da chiesa, e da camera* (1656). By 1703 Sebastien de Brossard defines the distinction of style based upon function in his *Dictionnaire de musique.* This distinction is mainly that the *sonata da chiesa* is the more serious composition of the two and employs fugal and other abstract movements having only tempo markings, while the *sonata da camera* usually consists of an introductory prelude followed by a series of dances in the same key—a dance suite. Despite this seemingly clear delineation of *da chiesa* and *da camera,* the truth is that the ensemble sonatas after 1660 indicate an increasing overlapping of styles, and after 1700 the stylistic distinction almost disappears.

It was during the period from about 1640 to 1690 that the *sonata da chiesa* and the *sonata da camera* became relatively well-defined musical categories, and the sonata achieved its "classic" design, largely as a result of the works of Legrenzi, Cazzati, and G. B. Vitali—thereafter mainly to be refined by Corelli. Other significant composers of this time are Torelli, G. M. Bononcini, Colombi, T. A. Vitali, Bassani, A. Veracini, Young, Biber, Walther, Krieger, Erlebach, Reinken, Rosenmüller, Buxtehude, Purcell, Ravenscroft, Couperin, Schenk, and Colista.

Northern Italy is the leader in the process of codifying the characteristics that tend to identify the mid-Baroque ensemble or trio sonata. The two most significant figures in this process appear to have been Mauritio Cazzati and Giovanni Legrenzi, who moved in the same circles in Bergamo between 1653 and 1657. Legrenzi published his first book of sonatas in 1655, seven years after Cazzati had published his second, and Cazzati's conception of the sonata seems to have had a strong influence on Legrenzi's instrumental works. In 1657, Cazzati moved to Bologna to become the head of the musical forces at San Petronio. Here he established a center for instrumental music. Both Bologna and Modena soon became primary focal points for the composition, publication and performance of instrumental ensemble music, and ensemble sonatas in particular. This geographical center has been called the "Bolognese School" of instrumental music, but the more appropriate term, "Emilian School," after the province of Emilia in which both Modena and Bologna are located, has now been accepted by most music historians. This school of composition of instrumental ensemble music includes virtually all the significant Italian composers listed above, from Cazzati to Corelli.

The overall structure of the *sonata da chiesa,* which generally utilizes strings plus keyboard *continuo,* consists of a group of movements, usually three to five, contrasting in texture, speed, rhythm, and character. These movements are commonly paired—a slow homophonic movement (introductory in character) with a fast contrapuntal movement. This is the basis of Corelli's classic S F S F four-movement structure. The clear presence of functional harmony and tonality provides musical direction, away from and returning to the tonic, as well as a means for the unification of individual movements and the entire sonata.

The *sonata da chiesa* employs three basic types of movements from which others were derived. The first type is the fast, duple meter, fugal or *canzona* movement which is described by William S. Newman as "a series of complete or incomplete expositions of a single subject in several nearly related keys, bridged by modulatory episodes that progress by sequential motivic play on some element of that subject or its attendant counterpoint."[2] The episodes vary considerably in length and, as time progresses, reveal a consistent increase in the application of variation technique to the fragments of the subject which are utilized for episodic expansion. The impact of functional harmony and tonality is revealed particularly through the use of arpeggiated and triadic subjects, "tonal" answers, frequent cadencing, systematic sequential *fortspinnung* through a series of secondary dominants or dominant seventh chords

with a bass pattern of the circle of fifths, various bass patterns that progress through temporary tonal areas by disjunct or conjunct motion (as the *chaconne* bass), and occasional modulations to closely related keys.

The consistent expansion in length and sequential technique is also reflected in the changes that occur in the construction of subjects. A typical subject of a fugal movement in a sonata around 1650 (see the beginning of No. 19) would usually utilize some type of dactylic rhythm, repeated notes, a small number of motivic cells, and a rather lengthy line before cadence points would be reached. This type of subject is closely associated with the conservative *canzona.* The progressive type of subject, on the other hand, would generally begin with an upbeat, be divisible into phrases that would cadence according to functionally harmonic patterns, and would contain multiple motivic cells capable of being utilized for episodic expansion (see the beginning of No. 27).

The second type of movement is the slow, homophonic, duple meter movement with an affective character normally attained through the use of a homophonic or pseudo-contrapuntal texture, affective harmonies and melodic devices (chromaticism, suspension chains, cross-relations, *tremolo,* unprepared dissonances, etc.), and a melodic and harmonic design of periodic phrase structure that moves quickly, via transitory modulations to closely related keys, from the tonic to the dominant or relative major and back to the tonic. These movements are usually in some type of binary or ternary form, and they appear to have originated as introductory to the major movements, before expanding into independent movements on their own.

The third type of movement is the triple meter movement, fast or slow, which reveals *sonata da camera* elements through the use of dance rhythms, as the *gagliarda, sarabanda,* and *corrente,* as well as periodic phrase structure and *concertante* writing. Although there are frequent imitative entries, these entries are not indicative of a contrapuntal approach but rather of a brief pseudo-counterpoint which quickly dissolves into conjunct melodic lines in parallel thirds and sixths. These lines frequently incorporate diatonic sequences which control their extension.

The internal organization of these movements is based on melodic phrases which briefly move, through sequences, to related tonal areas. Each succeeding phrase often derives a melodic pattern from the initial phrase and continues the existing sequence, or begins a new one. These movements thus

---

[2] William S. Newman, *The Sonata in the Baroque Era* (Chapel Hill: University of North Carolina Press, 1959), p. 82.

consist of a number of varied melodic ideas extended through sequential expansion and yet unified by similar melodic materials and functional tonality.

In addition, there are frequent occasions where each melodic line is given soloistic opportunities and the *concertante* style is emphasized, as may be seen in Torelli's 1686 sonata collection. This *concertante* emphasis leads to the concerto.

The use of typical dance rhythm formulae, such as the *hemiola* and the $\frac{3}{2}$ organization of music written in $\frac{3}{4}$, is also frequent in these movements. These formulae are generally related to the *corrente* and *gagliarda*. Furthermore, closely associated with the third type of movement is the fast, compound meter movement in $\frac{6}{8}$ or $\frac{12}{8}$ employing *gigue* rhythms, occasional binary dance forms, and a pulsating meter. These movements ordinarily are used as the final movement of the sonata.

The *sonata da camera,* or dance suite, was also based on a slow-fast combination of dances, plus an occasional free movement reflecting the inclusion of *da chiesa* elements. At the midpoint of the seventeenth century the dance groupings and suites contained Italian dances almost exclusively, such as the *gagliarda, balletto,* aria, *giga, corrente, allemanda,* and *zoppa.* By the end of the seventeenth century, however, French dances became increasingly fashionable and the gavotte, minuet, *bourree,* and *branle* became common members of the *sonata da camera.*

Stylistically, the Italian dances in the late seventeenth century *sonata da camera* are less stereotyped than the French dances. The symmetry of the patterned four-bar phrases of the French dances occurs infrequently in the Italian dances. In the common bipartite structure with repeats, asymmetric sections were the norm in the Italian dances, usually with the second section extended for modulatory interest. The internal structure of the Italian dances varies between homophonic, periodic phrase structure, and contrapuntal sequential expansion. The dances are linked tonally and, frequently, through melodic material; their order and number was not clearly defined, but by the 1680's a common pattern for the *sonata da camera* was prelude, *allemanda, courante* or *sarabande,* and a *gigue, gavotte,* or *sarabande* as the finale.

The employment of contrapuntal texture in the free movements that entered the *sonata da camera* clearly indicates the infusion of *da chiesa* elements into the *da camera* category. This infusion continued into the eighteenth century to such a degree that the designations of *da chiesa* and *da camera* were dropped.

Instrumental Ensemble Music around 1700.

By 1700 the ensemble sonata had reached the apex of its popularity, and from this point its story is one of gradually decreasing importance, as opposed to the rapidly increasing significance of the solo sonata and the concerto. This shift is reflected in the stylistic features of the ensemble sonata around 1700, which indicate two general trends—the strong conservative tradition continuing in the path of the Emilian School through Corelli's students and works, and the progressive tendencies modernizing the sonata in ways that emphasize the *concertante* direction. These stylistic directions indicate only propensities and not exclusiveness, for there was a consistently large degree of overlapping between these styles, and, furthermore, the composers presented their individual solutions through the manipulation of whichever style was appropriate to their purposes. Nevertheless, some of the primary features that tend to identify the progressive stylistic directions are: a total synthesis of the church and chamber sonata characteristics; the beginning of the general reduction of movements to three (especially F S F or S F F); the added use of *da capo* and *rondo* designs; some use of moderate speeds and ornamented melody; less counterpoint and more virtuosic writing for the upper part, through figuration, passagework, and optional second violin parts; more regular and balanced phrase lengths than before; reliance on the continuous, simple, and strong accents, related to dance rhythms, to provide a powerful and pulsating metric drive; the use of rhythmic *accelerandi* and *decelerandi,* syncopation, and dotted rhythms; the frequent use of "running" bass lines; the slowing down of harmonic rhythm when a *concertante* part is active; an occasional longer tonal plane; expansion of harmonic vocabulary through the increased use of Neapolitan sixth, the augmented sixth, and diminished seventh chords, as well as their inversions, for expressive purposes; affective titles; and a general stress on pathos, especially in the slower movements. Many of these traits clearly indicate close relationships to the solo sonata and concerto.

The solo sonata, although not as popular as the ensemble sonata, was composed throughout the seventeenth century, as the examples in the Wasielewski collection will testify (see Nos. 13, 22, 24, and 35). In addition to the solo violin sonata—whose primary function was to provide an arena for virtuosic display of the technical capabilities of the instrument—there arose another type of soloistic sonata, well illustrated in the Emilian School's particular predilection for solo and ensemble trumpet sonatas with string ensemble accompaniments. The earliest appearance of this type of work seems to be in Mauritio Cazzati's ensemble sonata collection of 1665 (Opus 35). The trumpet sonata was particularly popular in Bologna where it became closely identified with the festivities of the basilica of San Petronio. Some other composers who wrote trumpet sonatas are G. Torelli, G. Jachini, and Domenico Gabrieli. The importance of these trumpet sonatas lies in the fact that they combined two Baroque concepts—the *concertato* and *concertante* styles—in a new manner. The trumpet sonata returned to the antiphonal *concertato* tradition through the regular alternation between trumpet soloists and the accompanying strings, while the soloistic trumpet writing emphasized a *concertante* influence which appears to be but an extension of the solo sonata.

It was not a large leap to move from a solo violin plus *basso continuo* or from a trio sonata to solo or duet trumpet plus the trio sonata ensemble. Furthermore, the next step leads to the concerto, where a solo instrument or trio sonata group would act as a *concertino* with and against a string ensemble. The actual birth of the concerto is still shrouded in mystery, but Alessandro Stradella is generally given credit for the first *concerto grosso,* which was written between 1670 and 1680 as part of a group of *sinfonie: Sinfonia a violini e bassi a concertino e concerto grossi distinti.* This concerto, however, gives the *concertino* very little soloistic material and should, perhaps, be considered a major predecessor of the concerto. In any case, Guiseppi Torelli is perhaps the most famous composer associated with the origin of the concerto (see Nos. 25 and 26).

Both Torelli and Stradella are closely linked to the Emilian School of instrumental composition. Torelli (1658–1709) was born in Verona but studied, composed, performed, and lived most of his life in Bologna, while Stradella very likely studied in Modena with Uccellini and G. M. Bononcini, and was familiar with Bolognese instrumental music. In short, the concerto appears to have arisen as a product of the Emilian School.

The primary contributions of the seventeenth century to the history of instrumental music was the creation, development and codification of the Baroque ensemble sonata, and the creation of the solo sonata, the solo concerto and the *concerto grosso.* Wasielewski's astute choice of musical selections offers the student of seventeenth century instrumental music a fine cross-section of the music of the century, as well as an excellent coverage of the development of the major instrumental categories of Baroque ensemble music.

John G. Suess

Case Western Reserve University
September, 1968

xii

BIBLIOGRAPHY

Barnes, Marysue. "The Trio Sonatas of Antonio Caldara." Ph. D. diss.: Florida State, 1960.

Bonta, Stephen. "The Church Sonatas of Giovanni Legrenzi." Ph. D. diss.: Harvard, 1964.

Brockhoff, Maria-Elisabeth. "Studien zur Struktur der italienischen und deutschen Triosonate im 17. Jahrhudert." Ph. D. diss.: Münster, 1944.

Brossard, Sebastien de. *Dictionnaire de musique,* 3rd ed. Amsterdam: Pierre Mortier, 1710.

Crocker, Eunice Chandler. "An Introductory Study of the Italian Canzona for Instrumental Ensembles and Its Influence upon the Baroque Sonata." Ph. D. diss.: Radcliff, 1943.

Dunn, Thomas D. "The Instrumental Music of Biagio Marini." Ph. D. diss.: Yale University, 1969.

Hutchins, Arthur. *The Baroque Concerto.* New York: Norton, 1961.

Klenz, William. *Giovanni Maria Bononcini of Modena.* Durham, North Carolina: Duke University Press, 1962.

McCrickard, Eleanor F. "Alessandro Stradella's Instrumental Music." Ph. D. diss.: University of North Carolina, 1971.

Meyer, Ernst. *Die Mehrestimmige Spielmusik des 17. Jahrhunderts in Nord- und Mitteleuropa.* Kassel: Bärenreiter, 1934.

Mishkin, Henry G. "The Solo Violin Sonata of the Bologna School," *The Musical Quarterly* XXIX/1 (January 1943), 92–112.

Nef, Karl. *Zur Geschichte der deutschen Instrumentalmusik in der zweiter Hälfte des 17. Jahrhunderts,* (BMIG), I, 5, (1902).

Newman, William S. *The Sonata in the Baroque Era.* Chapel Hill: University of North Carolina Press, 1959.

Norton, Richard E. "The Chamber Music of Giuseppe Torelli." Ph.D. diss.: Northwestern University, 1967.

Riemann, Hugo. "Die Triosonaten der Generalbass-Epoche," *Präludien und Studien,* III, (1901), 129–56.

—————. *Handbuch der Musikgeschichte,* II, Part 2. Leipzig: Breitkopf & Härtel, 1922.

Rowen, Ruth. *Early Chamber Music.* New York: King's Crown Press, 1949; reprint, New York: Da Capo Press, 1973.

Sartori, Claudio. *Bibliographia della musica strumentale italiana.* Florence: Olschki, 1952.

Schenk, Erich. "Osservazione sulla scuola instrumentale modenesa nel seicento," *Atti e memorie della accademia di scienze, lettere, e arti di Modena,* Ser. V, Vol. X (1952), 3–29.

—————, ed. *Die italienische Triosonate.* Cologne: Arno Volk-Verlag, 1954.

Schering, Arnold. *Geschichte des Instrumentalkonzerts.* Leipzig: Breitkopf & Härtel, 1927

—————. "Zur Geschichte der Solosonate in der ersten Hälfte des 17. Jahrhunderts," *Riemann-Festschrift* (Leipzig: M. Hesses, 1909), 309–24.

Schlossberg, Artur. *Die italienische Sonata für mehrere Instrumente im 17. Jahrhundert.* Heidelberg: Heidelberger Studien, 1932.

Suess, John G. "Giovanni Battista Vitali and the Sonata da chiesa." Ph. D. diss.: Yale, 1963.

Swenson, Milton A. "The Four-Part Italian Ensemble Ricercar from 1540 to 1619." Ph.D. diss.: Indiana University, 1970.

NOTES

Wasielewski's edition is surprisingly accurate when one considers that such a modern convenience and ever-present checking device as microfilm was not available to him. There are only two particular problematic situations that occur in his almost flawless transcriptions. The first is in No. 10, Marini's *Romanesca per violino solo e basso se piace,* which is obviously incorrectly barred in the four parts. The editor apparently misread the C sign to mean $\frac{4}{4}$ instead of simply indicating the duple mensuration, and the parts should be barred in $\frac{3}{2}$ or $\frac{3}{1}$ to clarify the *romanesca* melody in the bass line (see correctly measured version in notes for No. 10, below). The second situation occurs in measure eighteen of Mont'Albano's *Sinfonia a duoi violini e basso* (No. 14), where Wasielewski put a question mark. The parallel seconds that occur on the last two beats of the measure do indeed occur in the print found in the Bolognese Conservatory, and are either an original misprint or the composer's desired dissonances. Since no satisfactory solution is apparent, the measure was wisely left alone by Wasielewski. The only changes that he made from the original prints are some obvious printer's errors, such as missing rests, incorrect note values, and misplaced figures which were corrected without comment.

Nos. 1, 2 • Florentio Maschera: *Canzoni da sonare*

The instrumental *canzona* has its stylistic prototype in the polyphonic *chanson.* Early versions of the *canzona* date back to the fifteenth century. By the late sixteenth century, the *canzona* began to be considered an independent instrumental category. Florentio Maschera's *canzoni* reflect this transitional stage between strict adherence to the polyphonic *chanson* style and newer instrumental conceptions. Both the *canzoni* reproduced here utilize such typical *chanson* features as sectionalization, points of imitation, conjunct melodic lines, diatonic harmony, the Flemish style of polyphonic texture, and some form of the characteristic dactylic rhythmic formula (especially in *La Capriola).*

These two *canzoni,* nevertheless, also demonstrate a considerable difference in their formal conception. *Canzona* No. 2 has a close affinity to the conventional type of *canzona:* its sections reveal more distinct changes in thematic and rhythmic materials than do those in No. 1. *La Capriola,* on the other hand, displays a structural scheme of: *a a a'a'* coda, in which there is basically only one subject (*a*), which is only slightly altered by sequence (*a'*). This work reveals the composer's concern for establishing an abstract formal design based more upon principles of construction intrinsically associated with musical logic, such as repetition and variation, rather than an organization stemming from a textually oriented tradition.

Source: *Libro Primo de canzoni da sonare, a quattro voci. Di Florentio Maschera organista nel duomo di Brescia. Novamente con ogni diligenza ristampate* (Venice, 1593). Wasielewski's reference to this reprint as the second edition of this collection is inaccurate. The original edition is believed to have been printed in 1582, and was reprinted in 1584, 1588, 1593, 1607, and 1621.

No. 3 • Giovanni Gabrieli: *Canzona per sonar. Primi toni*

This *canzona* by Giovanni Gabrieli serves to illustrate the impact of the Venetian polychoral school upon the *canzona per sonar.* Outside of the use of the dactylic rhythmic formula and diatonic writing, there is little resemblance to the polyphonic *chanson.* The Flemish polyphony has given way largely to chordal concept, and the pseudo-imitation serves mainly to link the entrances of the antiphonal choirs. The acoustical characteristics of St. Mark's undoubtedly encouraged the tonal harmony clearly displayed by the movement of the bass lines in the two equal choirs. The use of abstract formal structure emphasizes the inventiveness of the composer; the alternating duple and triple meter provides a sectional structure of A B C B D, where the A section can be further divided into: *a a a'a'.* The use of triple meter sections, uncommon in the multisectional *canzona,* is used for structural unification in a recapitulation manner. The primary emphasis is, nevertheless, on sonorities, their combinations and contrasts as well as directionality.

Source: *Sacrae symphoniae* (Venice, 1597).

No. 4 • Giovanni Gabrieli: *Sonata pian e forte. Alla quarta bassa*

This unique work comes from the same collection of sacred works as No. 3.

It is the only sonata in the collection, and one of only three works in which the composer has clearly delineated the instrumentation. In this composition, each choir consists of three trombones, with a *cornetto* playing the soprano line in one choir and a *violino* playing a similar part in the other choir. As the title indicates, the concern for sonorities overshadows everything else in this sonata, for this work is the earliest extant ensemble composition to indicate the dynamic contrasts of *piano* and *forte.* This invention provides the basis for the total substance of the work. Structurally, there seem to be no sections that have any thematic relationships, and it is the dynamic as well as antiphonal contrasts that unify the work.

Source: *Sacrae symphoniae* (Venice, 1597).

Nos. 5, 6 • Adriano Banchieri: *Fantasie*

The early seventeenth century *fantasia* with its imitative polyphony resembled the *ricercar* and *canzona* more closely than anything else, but the term was still applied rather freely. These two Banchieri fantasies are part of his collection *Fantasie overo canzoni alla francese per suonare nell'organo et altri stromenti musicali a quattro voci,* whose title indicates the confusion between the fantasy and the *canzona* and the possible performance either by organ or organ and/or other instruments. This also explains the title of No. 5, *Fantasia in Eco movendo un Registro,* which refers to the echo technique, requiring two different registrations on the organ. Banchieri, who was a colleague of Giovanni Gabrieli at St. Mark's from 1588 to 1595, employs the *piano* and *forte* dynamic contrasts only in the chordal middle section of this *fantasia.* The two triple meter outer sections are in an imitative polyphonic style revealing an A B A form for the total work. The *fantasia* No. 6 follows the traditional sectionalized structure based on points of imitation, and uses the dactylic *canzona* rhythmic formula in the first subject. This *fantasia* uses two themes in an A B A B structure. Both of these works reflect an abstract formal structure.

Source: *Fantasie overo canzoni alla francese per suonare nell'organo et altri stromenti musicali a quattro voci, nuovamente reviste, & ristampate* (Venice, 1603). This collection was originally printed in 1596.

No. 7 • Giovanni Gabrieli: *Sonata con tre violini*

The sonata at the beginning of the seventeenth century is a category for experimentation, as was already seen in No. 4. The *Sonata con tre violini* plus a *basso se piace*—an organ bass plus string bass *ad libitum*—displays a step into the Baroque era. The bass line, with its emphasis on longer note values and little use of thematic material, acts and functions as a harmonic line in most of the piece, although it still maintains its melodic character. The three violins plus bass also emphasize the trio texture throughout much of the work. Structurally, the three violins have imitative entries of short thematic material. When the melodic lines are extended, they reveal a concern for a technique of expansion that later led to one of the fundamental devices for Baroque instrumental composition—the sequence. Gabrieli also employs the dialogue technique with sequential expansion.

Source: *Canzoni e sonate* (Venice, 1615).

No. 8 ● Giovanni Gabrieli: *Canzona*

This six-voice *canzona,* also from Gabrieli's 1615 collection of *canzoni* and *sonate* reveals the combination of various formal considerations to provide an abstract structure of similarity and difference. Gabrieli combines variation technique with a *ritornello* structure to provide a relatively sophisticated design: $a\,b\,a^1\,b\,a^2\,b\,a^3\,b\,b\,a^4$, plus a coda. The traditional multisectional concept is clear, but these sections now consist of only two different ideas unified by variation and repetition. The duple meter *"a"* section is always in a polyphonic or dialogue style, while the triple meter *"b"* sections are always chordal. The trio texture is very prominent—generally the pair of violins or the two middle voices with one of the trombones.

Source: *Canzoni e sonate* (Venice, 1615).

No. 9 ● Biagio Marini: Dances from *Opus III* (1620)

a. *La Martinenga Corente a 3*

This early seventeenth century instrumental version of the Italian *corente* reveals the binary structure and chordal texture generally associated with such dances at this time. The trio texture is clear, and the basically four-bar phrases of the first section are extended by sequences in the second section. The clear harmonic scheme of I V I is particularly apparent in the first section. The oc-

casional use of hemiola rhythms marks the beginning of rhythmic manipulation.

b. *Il Pricilino Balletto & Corente*

This combination of a duple plus a triple meter dance, based upon the variation principle and identical key for unity, indicates a typical Renaissance grouping, but the trio texture and the use of sequential expansion point toward a Baroque concept.

Source: *Arie, madrigali, et corenti a 1, 2, 3. Op. III* (Venice, 1620).

No. 10 ● Biagio Marini: *Romanesca per violino solo e Basso se piace*

This set of solo violin variations over an optional bass line reveals a truly monodic approach to instrumental composition. For the organization of his harmonies, Marini used the *romanesca* melody, an old dance melody that became one of the standard repertory of melodies suitable for controlling the succession of harmonies. This allowed melodic variation over a systematically organized harmonic foundation, and since the *romanesca* melody included the I IV V I progression, it also encouraged the establishment of a functional harmonic scheme. The binary structure of the *romanesca* melody also provides the basic bipartite structure of each variation, with V and I cadences at the end of the first and second sections respectively. Although Wasielewski had published this work with the original barring, we must agree with suggested grouping made by Willi Apel in his *Historical Anthology of Music* (Cambridge, Mass., 1950), No. 199, Vol. II. The triple rhythm groupings make musical sense and the *romanesca* melody (+) becomes apparent. The beginnings of idiomatic violin writing is also observable in this work, especially in the third part.

Source: *Arie, madrigali, et corenti a 1, a 2, a 3. Op. III* (Venice, 1620).

Biagio Marini: *Romanesca per violino e Basso se piace*

This is a more correctly measured version of Marini's composition which appears on pages 18–19. Only the *romanesca* has been transcribed in its entirety, since the corrections called for in the *gagliarda* and *corente* are of a nature similar to those incorporated in this movement.

No. 11 • Carlo Farina: Fragment from his *Capriccio stravagante*

This fragment of the cantus part of Carlo Farina's "whimsical caprice" illustrates both the technical virtuosity and the idiomatic violin writing that had been attained in the early seventeenth century. The idiomatic passagework plus the virtuosic use of multiple stops and such special effects as *col legno,* syncopated slurring, and to bow in the manner of a *lira,* all demonstrate the technical achievements of the performers and the inventiveness of the composer. The composition consists of short, repeated sections, each section employing sound effects for the purpose of imitating sounds associated with other musical instruments (such as fife, *lira,* and "small, soldier's flute") as well as sounds imitating domestic animals (such as cat, dog, hen, and cock).

Source: *Paduanen, Gagliarden, Couranten, Französichen. Arien, benehenst einem kurtz-weiligen Quodlibet, von allerhand seltzamen Inventionen* (Dresden, 1627).

Nos. 12, 13 • Giovanni Battista Fontana: *Sonatas*

Both the trio sonata and the solo sonata are from the only published collection of Fontana's sonatas—an opus which appeared eleven years after his death. They identify the early concept of the sonata as the amalgamation of *canzona* characteristics with the more idiomatic violin writing based upon the ornamental monodic style. These multi-sectional compositions employ a succession of sections using contrasting rhythms and textures, either chordal or contrapuntal. Violinistic passagework is also utilized in some sections. Both works reflect a growing interest in motivic expansion, especially through sequential dialogue. In the trio sonata, the bass line usually takes an active melodic part when there is contrapuntal activity, while in the solo sonata the bass line becomes much more of a partner to the violin solo, particularly through the dialogue technique. Written-out ornamentation, especially at cadence points, is prominent in these sonatas, and indicates that the performance conventions had not crystallized as yet. Fontana's solo sonatas are among the earliest for the violin.

Source: *Sonate a 1, 2, 3, per il violino, o cornetto, fagotto, chitarone, violoncino o simile altro istromento* (Venice, 1641).

No. 14 • Bartolomeo Mont'albano: *Sinfonia a duoi violini e basso,* called *"Castelletti"*

The term *sinfonia* had no particular meaning in the early seventeenth century, and was generally equivalent to sonata or even *canzòna.* In the original printing, the *sinfonia "Castelletti"* is actually scored for two violins plus trombone and organ for the bass part, although Wasielewski only indicates two violins and bass. This multisectional work consists of three large sections with contrasting rhythms and textures, but each of the two duple meter sections may easily be separated into subsections. Points of imitation plus an active melodic bass line emphasize the *canzona* tradition, while the more homophonic sections and the use of sequential dialogue technique based on the circle of fifths emphasize the new monodic directions in instrumental writing. Mont'albano was a Bolognese composer who spent much of his life in Palermo, Sicily.

Source: *Sinfonie ad uno, e doi violini, a doi e trombone, con il partimento per l'organo, con alcune a quattro viole* (Palermo, 1629).

No. 15 • Gregorio Allegri: *Symphonia a 4, duoi violini, alto e basso viola*

This composition, which was used as a musical illustration by Athanasius Kircher in his *Musurgia universalis,* reveals the application of the term *symphonia* to a conservative instrumental style, strongly rooted in the *canzona* tradition. The multisectional structure based largely upon contrasting points of imitation is reminiscent of English consort music, contemporary to Allegri's work. The polyphonic texture, the use of the dactylic rhythm in the first section, and the melodic orientation of the bass line emphasize the *canzona* character of this piece. The triple meter section with its accent on trio texture and parallel movement indicates the direction toward the new instrumental style, but even here there is much contrapuntal movement. Allegri was a Roman composer who concerned himself mainly with sacred vocal music.

Source: Athanasius Kircher, *Musurgia universalis* (Rome, 1650).

Nos. 16, 17 • Tarquinio Merula: *Canzoni a tre*

The rather experimental nature of the trio *canzona*-sonata category is particularly evident in these two *canzoni a tre* of Merula. Despite their being called canzoni, they differ little from the canzoni in Merula's 1637 collection, *Canzoni, overo sonate concertate per chiesa, e camera, libro terzo* (Opus XII, Venice, 1637). The 1637 collection also indicates that these *canzoni* were equally useful for either church or chamber, as is also most likely the case for the examples: *Canzon detta la Cancelliera* and *Canzon detta la Visconta.* Both these examples exhibit the usual multi-sectional structure, but now each section is becoming unified as a result of generally employing only one basic theme within it. The contrasting sections now begin to show more precise differentiations than before through the use of more clearly separate types of textures and tempo markings. The bass line consists of a bass voice which frequently participates in the polyphonic sections and doubles the keyboard instrument in homophonic sections. The thematic materials no longer use the dactylic *canzona* rhythm; they consist of complete ideas with clear cadences, but no consistent pattern of imitative entries exists in the contrapuntal sections as yet. The *Canzon detta la Visconta* opens with the theme and its inversion. The harmonic vocabulary is increasingly varied, especially through the frequent use of seventh chords and suspensions. Suspension chains are also becoming a prominent means of providing the basis for sequential expansion. No. 16 reveals that idiomatic violin writing also begins to take on some functional aspects, as in the two-octave opening theme, the sequential passage in octave leaps, and the *tremolo* passage. The *tremolo* probably was performed either as a *vibrato* or in the modern manner. These characteristics display the progressive tendencies of the trio sonata at this time.

Source: *Il secondo libro delle canzoni da suonare a tre, duoi violini, e basso, con il basso generale* (Opus IX, Venice, 1639).

Nos. 18, 19 • Massimiliano Neri: *Canzon del terzo tuono and Sonata*

Although these two compositions have different titles and come from two separate collections (the *canzona* is in Neri's 1644 collection and the sonata in his 1651 collection), they reveal such similar conceptions of structure and style that the titular distinctions are virtually meaningless. The arbitrary nomenclature is also apparent from the titles of the collections—one is called *Sonate e canzone...* (1644) and the other simply *Sonate...* (1651). Neri also makes no differentiation between church and chamber music, since his 1644 collection clearly indicates that his works are to be played *"in chiesa, e in camera."* Both the *canzona* and sonata are four-voice works for two violins and viola, and differ only in that the composer specifically designates a viola or bassoon for the bass part in the *canzona*. Both compositions reveal a string quartet arrangement except for the added keyboard *continuo* (which acts only as a *basso seguente*). These two multisectional works display some expanded duple and triple meter fugal movements which are frequently separated by short homophonic cadential sections. Although there are tempo indications, they are more consistently employed in the sonata than in the *canzona*. Of particular significance are the progressive ideas in the fugal movements, which demonstrate clear fugal subjects, specific exposition structure, a totally monothematic conception, true fugal episodes, and a lucid conception of tonality, despite the references to the church modes. The thematic fragmentation and episodic expansion is especially impressive. Another unusual feature is the *concertato* alternation between the violins and the lower strings, which reminds one of the earlier polychoral style. On the other hand, Neri still clings to the use of repeated-note subjects, a leftover from the *canzona* tradition.

Source: No. 18, *Sonate e canzone a quattro da sonarsi con diversi stromenti in chiesa, e in camera con alcune correnti pure a quattro, che si ponno sonare a tre, e a due ancora, lasciando fuori le parti di mezzo* (Opus I, Venice, 1644); No. 19, *Sonate da sonarsi con varii stromenti a tre sino a dodeci* (Opus II, Venice, 1651).

No. 20 • Massimiliano Neri: Fragment from a Sonata for three flutes, two violins, *violetta,* and *tiorba* or viola.

This fragment comes from the same collection as No. 19. This collection is for various combinations of instruments, from *a tre sino a dodeci,* and the composer specifically designates the parts for *"violino, viola, fagotto, basso, viola da brazzo, cornetti, tromboni, violetta, teorba, flauti."* This fragment for two choirs is scored for three flutes, two violins, *violetta,* and *tiorba* or *viola di basso*. The use of alternating choirs in the polychoral tradition is expanded by the use of the solo trio of strings, and foreshadows the future concerto. The fragment has a basically trio fugal texture plus continuo.

Source: *Sonate da sonarsi con varii stromenti a tre sino a dodeci* (Opus II, Venice, 1651).

Nos. 21, 22 • Biagio Marini: Two sonatas

Both these sonatas come from the same collection, Marini's Opus 22 (1655). This collection is one of the first to differentiate clearly the sonata according to its function in fact, as well as in the title—*diversi generi di sonate, da chiesa, e da camera....* The chamber sonatas result from a grouping of dances, and the church sonatas consist of a group of contrasting movements, with a heavy emphasis on counterpoint. Both of these sonatas (Nos. 21 and 22) are *sonate*

xviii

da chiesa and consist of various movements contrasting in texture, tempo, and rhythm; and both are basically trio sonatas with the "sonata for violin and bass" differing from the other mainly in having the bass part substituting for the second violin. The *basso continuo* now usually functions as an independent bass line, except in No. 22, where it is closely related to the active bass line. These two sonatas also reflect the general tendency to reduce the number of sections to range from three to five movements, where one movement is generally in a triple meter. Marini also employs the technique of separating the imitative entries far enough to create the impression of soloistic alternation, since the counterpoint may not continue in the voice with the initial entry. The thematic materials are idiomatically conceived for instruments, and Marini frequently uses themes with up-beat rhythms. The composer's structural concern is particularly evident in No. 22, where each major movement is clearly delineated by the terms *prima parte, secunda parte,* and *terza parte.* In these works, Marini reflects the initial stages of a major concern of the middle Baroque: the structural codification of the ensemble and solo sonata based upon a functional conception of tonality.

Source: *Per ogni sorte d'stromento* [sic] *musicale diversi generi di sonate, da chiesa, e da camera, a due, tre, a a quattro* (Opus XXII, Venice, 1655).

No. 23 • Giovanni Legrenzi: Sonata for two violins and bass, *La Cornara*

Legrenzi and his elder contemporary, if not teacher, Mauritio Cazzati are two of the most significant names associated with the structural codification of the mid-seventeenth century trio sonata. This trio sonata, *La Cornara,* was published in Bergamo in 1654, when Cazzati was also there. This *sonata da chiesa* identifies some of the major characteristics of this musical category at the mid-century point. The structure consists of three main movements: two duple meter movements enclosing the middle triple meter movement, with the last movement beginning with a homophonic introductory *adagio* before a shortened recapitulation of the initial movement ends the work. The scheme is therefore *a b (c a')* and the tempo indications would be Fast Fast (Slow Fast). There is a clear separation of melodic and harmonic function between the violins and the *basso continuo.* The functional harmonies and tonality help organize the movements through a cadence scheme of *d, a, f,* and *d,* with the entire work clearly in *d* minor. The fugal subjects outline the tonic and dominant triads, and the episodic expansion employs sequence through a part

of the circle of fifths or fourths. Not only do the monothematic fugal movements clearly present an exposition structure plus episodes, but Legrenzi also employs a very strict canonic technique in the triple meter section. Of particular importance is the contraction of many sections to fewer sections which have been extended in length, the idiomatic violin writing without the virtuosic techniques that were found in earlier works, and the emphasis on functional tonality as a structural controlling agent.

Source: *Sonate a due, e tre* (Opus II, Venice, 1655).

No. 24 • Giovanni Legrenzi: *Sonata a 5, "La Fugazza"*

Unlike his trio sonata (No. 23), this five voice sonata, which was published while Legrenzi was in Ferrara, reflects the multisectional *canzona* tradition more than the progressive sonata. The many small sections and the brief subjects used in the imitative counterpoint accent the *canzona* influence, but the use of brief *adagio* introductions, tempo indications, the emphasis on chord tones in the themes, and the unification of all the major sections through subjects beginning with the leap of a fourth tend to remind one of the progressive style of this work. This type of work, a new style in an old framework, occurs sporadically during the mid-seventeenth century.

Source: *Sonate a 2, 3, 5, e 6 istromenti, Libro terza* (Opus 8, Venice, 1663).

No. 25 • Giovanni Battista Vitali: *Balletto a tre* and *Corrente*

With the generation of G. B. Vitali, a pupil of Cazzati, the primary characteristics of the trio sonata, both *da chiesa* and *da camera,* achieve codification. Vitali's first published collection separated the *balletti* from the *correnti,* but this example clearly reveals how these dances were probably combined on a basis of similar tonality, thematic material, and cadence patterns. Each dance has a binary structure, and each section has a cadence pattern of tonic minor to relative major and back to tonic minor. The phrase structures are not regular and begin with an anacrusis. The separation of melodic and harmonic lines is absolute, and the parallel writing in the violins displays no counterpoint whatsoever. The violin technique is modest—the obvious emphasis is on unifying structural factors. The combination of a duple meter dance followed by a triple meter dance is a tradition emanating from the early Renaissance.

Source: *Correnti, e balletti da camera a due violini, col suo basso continuo per spinetta, o violone* (Opus I, Bologna, 1666).

No. 26 • Giovanni Battista Vitali: *Sonata a due violini col suo basso continuo per l'organo*

This trio *sonata da chiesa* displays many of the common features associated with this musical category in the last half of the seventeenth century. The structure clearly shows the alternation of homophonic and contrapuntal movements, a tempo design that is probably S F S F, the use of a variety of rhythms, the trio sonata texture of two melodic lines supported by the harmonic bass line, and a totally tonal conception. In addition, the harmonic rhythm begins to move more quickly than in earlier sonatas. In the fugal movement, the expositions are clearly presented, the subject has a tonal answer, the subjects are triadically conceived, the sequential episodes are commonplace, and the up-beat subjects are idiomatic to the violin. Finally, the $\frac{6}{4}$ and $\frac{12}{8}$ movements reflect the absorption of dance rhythms generally reserved for the *sonata da camera.* This is especially clear in the *gigue* rhythm in the last movement.

Source: *Sonate a due violini col suo basso continuo per l'organo* (Opus II, Bologna, 1667).

No. 27 • Giovanni Battista Vitali: *Sonata a due Violini e organo,* called *"La Graziani"*

This four movement (F F S F) *sonata da chiesa* reflects a variety of techniques which later become part of the Baroque composer's vocabulary. The fragmentary subject of the fugal entries in the first movement clearly divides the subject into two balanced parts, and also provides the rich assortment of motivic materials for episodic expansion. The *largo* movement displays a soloistic approach to the presentation of thematic materials, before parallel writing continues the phrases through transitory modulations on the way to the dominant. The frequent use of $\frac{3}{2}$ rhythm in this movement reflects the typical *corrente* dance rhythm. Finally, the abbreviated subject material of the last movement provides a link to the first movement through the use of similar motives—the result being a loose type of recapitulation structure.

Source: *Sonate a due, tre, quattro, e cinque stromenti* (Opus V, Bologna, 1669).

No. 28 • Giovanni Battista Vitali: *Capriccio a 4, due violini, alto e violone,* called *"Capriccio detto il Molza"*

This singular work in Vitali's Opus V indicates the free type of composition associated with the term *capriccio* in the last half of the seventeenth century. It allows the composer to show his inventiveness, and here Vitali concentrates on working with suspension and dialogue sequence structures. Most of the piece employs descending bass lines which often outline a fourth, a fifth, or an octave. The suspension sequences help to maintain an equality of voices, although the piece is predominantly homophonic. Even in the final movement, which has imitative entries, the "subject" consists of a broken triad in sequence, and the resulting texture is mainly that of a four-part dialogue sequence. The work appears to have been experimental and this would account for the composer's choice of the title in a *sonata da chiesa* collection.

Source: *Sonate a due, tre, quattro, e cinque stromenti* (Opus V, Bologna, 1669).

No. 29 • Marco Uccellini: Two *Sinfonie* for solo violin and bass

Despite the reference to solo violin and bass, these two *sinfonie* may be performed by two or three violins and bass, if so desired. The title clearly indicates this option— "...with the addition of two other violin parts *ad libitum,* in order to be able to play *a* 2, *a* 3, and *a* 4 as one desires." The most likely explanation as to why the Wasielewski edition has only two violin parts over the bass line is that his source in the Brussels library has the parts for only two violins and *basso continuo.* Near the end of the seventeenth century the term *sinfonia* was often equivalent to sonata, or was applied to less conventional works. In our examples, the two *sinfonie* are program works with identifying labels, *La Suavissima* (the suavest) and *La Gran Battaglia* (the great battle). Both works display binary structure and programmatic effects: *La Suavissima* emphasizes the *legato* effect through slurs and ornamental trills, while the other employs *stile concitato.* One might be reminded of battle trumpets in the second section of *La Gran Battaglia,* which is constructed on the D major chord over a pedal point D, and the entire thematic material is based upon plain or ornamented versions of the D major arpeggio. Total unity is achieved through these means.

Source: *Sinfonie boscarecie a violino solo, e basso, con l'agiunta di due altri violini ad libitum, per poter sonare a due, a tre, e a quattro conforme piacera* (Opus VIII, Antwerp, 1669).

No. 30 • Giovanni Legrenzi: Sonata for two violins and bass (*a 3*, called *"La Rosetta"*

This three voice *sonata da chiesa* is from the same collection as No. 24, but tends to emphasize more progressive features than *La Fugazza.* There is only one main exposition in the *"canzona"* movement, the first movement, and the episodic expansion is extensive as well as limited to mainly one motive. The *adagio* movement employs counterpoint and is rather long. The four movement work has a F S F S design as well as a cadence and tonal pattern of *d F d d.* Of particular note is that the opening movement is in a compound meter—a truly unusual circumstance. Yet, conservative features are still visible: the employment of real fugal answers, the repeated note pattern for the theme in the triple meter movement, and the heavy melodic use of the bass line in the contrapuntal movements.

Source: *Sonate a due, tre, cinque, e sei stromenti, libro terzo* (Opus VIII, Bologna, 1671). This is a Bolognese reprint of the original Venetian edition of 1663.

No. 31 • Giovanni Battista Mazzaferrata: Sonata for two violins and bass

This *sonata da chiesa* may be characterized as a rather fresh approach to the category—a type of simplification that anticipates future stylistic directions. Formally, it consists of a typical four movement structure: two duple meter *"canzona"* movements framing a pseudo-contrapuntal triple meter movement, and a homophonic movement. The freshness, however, lies in the two-bar, or multiples of two-bar, phrase structure; the fragmentary subjects with fragmentary countersubjects that mesh rather than compete with each other; the chordally oriented thematic materials (such as broken triads), which tend to slow down the harmonic rhythm; and the general lengthening of all of the

movements. It is now conventional to have imitative entries dissolve into parallel thirds and sixths, or dialogue sequences.

Source: *Il primo libro delle sonate a due violini con un bassetto viole se piace* (Opus V, Bologna, 1674).

No. 32 • Giovanni Battista Bassani: *Balletto, corrente, giga, e sarabanda* for two violins and bass

Although there are two violin parts in this edition, the second violin is optional, and this work could be performed as a solo violin suite. This dance group is a *sonata da camera* and is part of a collection of twelve dance suites, all with the same pattern of *Balletto* (duple meter), *Corrente* (triple), *Giga* (compound duple), and *Sarabanda* (triple). The tempo pattern is S F F F with the *Sarabanda* always having a tempo marking of *Presto* or *Prestissimo.* The *Sarabanda* frequently has fast tempo markings in Italian seventeenth century instrumental ensemble music. This *sonata da camera* by Bassani is a group of dances in binary form with repeated sections. The dances are linked by being in the same basic tonality, with excursions to the relative major or minor dominant, and the thematic materials for all of the dances are derived from the *Balletto.* Periodic cadences organize the melodic structure. Although these dances are primarily homophonic in conception, imitative entries and some pseudo-counterpoint do occur—a feature that was particularly common in Vitali's dance suites. Harmonic considerations in the construction of thematic materials are of primary concern after the midpoint of the seventeenth century.

Source: *Balletti, correnti, gighe, e sarabande a violino e violone, overo spinetta, con il secondo violino a beneplacito* (Opus I, Bologna, 1677).

No. 33 • Giovanni Battista Bassani: Sonata for two violins, violoncello (*ad libitum*) and organ

This unusual work is from Bassani's only collection of *sonate da chiesa,* his Opus V (1683); the title for the collection is *"sinfonie"* while each individual composition is called *"suonata"*—a common confusion of terms in the late seventeenth century. The seven movements of this work, along with the rather independent use of the violoncello, which is optional (*"a beneplacito"*), reveal that the *sonata da chiesa* was still an experimental category. The design of this sonata is: *a b c d e d' e'*, which shows that this work was still conceived as a five-movement work, plus the addition of variations of the last two movements. These variations were apparently thought to be necessary for tonal purposes, since the scheme for the movements is basically: I, V, I, IV, IV, I, and I. In any case, the last two movements return to the tonic. The tempo scheme is the usual alternation of fast and slow movements: F S F S F S F. Bassani is particuarly noted for his relatively smooth and long melodic lines, and this is reflected in this sonata, where instrumental lines have many repeated notes and tend to weave around notes that are central to the harmony. Relative to what was usual for the time, very little motivic fragmentation occurs in this work. In the first movement, the fugal subject is based on instrumentally conceived lines over a chromatically falling bass line, and melodic extension immediately pre-empts the place where the fugal answer would normally occur.

Source: *Sinfonie a due, e tre instromenti, con il basso continuo per l'organo* (Opus V, Bologna, 1683).

No. 34 • Giovanni Battista Bassani: Sonata for two violins and bass

This *sonata da chiesa* is from the same collection as No. 33, and consists of fundamentally three large contrapuntal movements, alternating duple and triple meter, which are preceded by introductory slow sections—a common practice since 1650. In this case, however, each introductory *Grave* has a clear harmonic function, as the tonal scheme indicates: *Grave* (V), *Presto* (I), *Grave* (IV), *Allegro* (IV), *Grave* (V), and *Allegro* (I). The central *Grave* is the largest slow section, and even has imitative entries. In the contrapuntal movements, Bassani employs three-part counterpoint, with the bass line taking an active part in the imitative entries, but the main concern is the melodic line. The manipulation of the sequential subject of the ⁶₈ *Allegro* reflects the type of counterpoint where the fugal entries are almost lost as the parallel writing in thirds provides the continuity. This stylistic direction marks a clear departure from the tight contrapuntal web found in similar works by earlier composers, such as Vitali, Legrenzi, and others.

Source: *Sinfonie a due, e tre instromenti, con il basso continuo per l'organo* (Opus V, Bologna, 1683).

No. 35 • Giuseppi Torelli: Sonata for violin solo, violoncello *obbligato* and cembalo

This sonata, which is attributed to Torelli in a private collection in Dresden, reflects the composer's concern for the *concertante* conception—one of the major conceptions in the development of the late Baroque solo sonata and concerto. In this case, we have two solo instruments, the violin and the violoncello. The use of the cello for soloistic purposes began in Bologna in the last three decades of the seventeenth century. The first movement of this basically four-movement structure (F F S F) is something of a fanfare in the character of the familiar trumpet sonatas of the time. The long soloistic lines in the violin repeated by the cello are based on sequence and triadic outlines. The interruptions of the solo lines by the *adagio* cadence patterns only tend to organize the otherwise improvisational quality of this movement. The "contrapuntal" movements reveal a much greater concern for dialogue between the soprano and bass solo lines than for competitive individual lines. The virtuosic lines, the dialogue technique, and the suspension sequences are employed for expansion purposes over a slow-moving harmonic rhythm.

Source: Private collection in Dresden, according to Wasielewski.

No. 36 • Giuseppi Torelli: *Concerto con due violini che concertino soli*

This is a *concerto grosso* by one of the innovators of this category. The collection from which this selection comes was published posthumously and contains six solo concerti as well as six *concerti grossi*. The *concerto grosso* emphasizes the contrasts between a solo ensemble (*concertino*), which is a trio sonata group in this case, and the full ensemble (*ripieno*), which consists of two violins, alto viola, and *basso continuo*. The solo ensemble is treated in *concertante* fashion to allow the performer on each of the soprano instruments an opportunity to demonstrate his virtuosity. The selection cited here reveals an overall structure of three main movements (F S F), with only the last movement utilizing any counterpoint. The two fast movements depend heavily on the contrast of sonorities and functional harmonic movement as structural building blocks, while in the middle movement there is an emphasis on special effects and affective harmonies. In both of the fast movements there is a succession of alternations between *soli* and *tutti*, with the initial *tutti* establishing the key firmly and providing the thematic materials that are varied by the solo ensemble for its own display purposes. The four-voice fugal last movement demonstrates the relation between *tutti* (*t*) and *soli* (*s*) in terms of tonal movement. The alternating structure is: (*tst*) (*ststs*) (*tst*), where the first group establishes G major with the main thematic materials, the second group makes excursions to closely related keys with the passage-work materials initially presented by the *soli,* and the final group returns to both the theme and the key of G major. Besides the multiple stops and affective harmonies, the middle movement (*Adagio-Andante*) employs the term *ondeggiando,* which refers to the wavy motion of the violin bow that is necessary when the performer must play these particular multiple stops in quick succession. This is a virtuosic technique that seems to have been invented near the end of the seventeenth century. Again, it is the various types of sequence, especially in conjunction with dialogue technique, that provide the means for thematic and ornamental expansion.

Source: *Concerti grossi con una pastorale per il santissimo natale* (Opus VIII, Bologna, 1709).

No. 37 ● Antonio Veracini: *Sonata a tre*

This sonata is from Antonio Veracini's only published collection of *sonate da chiesa* and reveals the new emphasis on homophony and the virtual absence of any counterpoint. This work is also unusual in having three slow movements and only one fast movement, providing the following design: S S F S. The two *affettuoso,* or expressive, movements are both in an ‖:A:‖:B:‖ structure, where both parts employ cadences on the tonic, c minor. All movements but the *vivace* begin with upbeat formulae. All the movements are unified by some subtle similarities or resemblances. The incipits of each movement have strong family resemblances: the major cadence points all employ the same formula; the melodic phrases are usually elongated for apparently no reason other than, perhaps, building the tension which is to be released when the cadences are reached; and there is consistent emphasis on parallel writing, despite the crossing of the upper parts.

Source: *Sonate a tre, due violini, e violone, o arcileuto col basso per l'organo* (Opus I, Florence, 1692).

No. 38 ● Antonio Veracini: *Sonata da camera* for violin or *archlute* and cembalo

This work stems from a collection entitled *Sonate da camera,* but none of the movements have dance identifications attached to them, which is normal for the *sonata da chiesa.* There are, nevertheless, several movements which utilize dance rhythms in this suite. In addition, there are four movements based upon the classic model of the *sonata da chiesa;* a design of S F S F, with the two fast movements demonstrating more contrapuntal writing than was seen in Veracini's *sonata da chiesa* (No. 37), and even the slower movements utilize an occasional pseudo-contrapuntal texture. Finally, the usual bipartite dance structure is totally absent. The total conception of this work, then, reveals the large scale interchange of characteristics between the church and chamber sonata—an assimilation that had began already in the works of Vitali, Cazzati, and G. M. Bononcini. The individual movements again appear to have thematic links, perhaps with the exception of the *largo.* The idiomatic violin writing, the imitative counterpoint that melts into parallel and dialogue writing, the extensive sequential expansions, and the emphasis in the slow movements on faster harmonic movement and on a wider harmonic vocabulary all tend to demonstrate that Veracini's sonata is a polished product of a long and dynamic tradition of instrumental ensemble music in the seventeenth century.

Source: *Sonate da camera a due violino, e violone, o arcileuto, col basso per il cimbalo* (Opus III, Modona, 1696).

ANTHOLOGY OF INSTRUMENTAL MUSIC
FROM THE END OF THE SIXTEENTH
TO THE
END OF THE SEVENTEENTH CENTURY

Instrumentalsätze

vom Ende des XVI. bis Ende des XVII. Jahrhunderts

(als Musikbeilagen zu „Die Violine im XVII. Jahrhundert")

gesammelt und herausgegeben

von

Jos. Wilh. von Wasielewski.

Bonn, Max Cohen & Sohn,
1874.

Preis 3 Thlr. netto.

Lith. und gedr. von J. Bach, Bonn.

Inhalts-Verzeichnis.

No

I.—II. **Maschera** (Florentio) Canzon da sonare a 4 (1593) 1, 2
III. **Gabrieli** (Giov.) Canzon per sonar. Primi toni (1597) . . . 4
IV. **Gabrieli** (Giov.) Sonata pian e forte. Alla quarta bassa (1597) 7
V. **Banchieri** (Adriano) Fantasia in Eco movendo un Registro (1603) 10
VI. **Banchieri** (Adriano) Fantasia (1603) 12
VII. **Gabrieli** (Giov.) Sonata con tre Violini (1615) 13
VIII. **Gabrieli** (Giov.) Canzon a 6 (1615) 15
IX. **Marini** (Biagio) La Martinenga. Corente a 3. (Aus Opus 3, 1620) 17
X. **Marini** (Biagio) Romanesca per Violino solo e Basso se piace . 18
XI. **Farina** (Carlo) Bruchstücke aus dem „Canto" des „Capriccio stravagante" (1627) 19
XII. **Fontana** (Giov. Battista) Sonata a tre (gegen 1630) 21
XIII. **Fontana** (Giov. Battista) Sonata a Violino solo (gegen 1630) . 23
XIV. **Mont' Albano** (Bartolomeo) Sinfonia a duoi Violini e Basso (1629) 25
XV. **Allegri** (Gregorio) Symphonia a 4, [Duoi Violini, Alto & Basso di Viola] (Vor 1650, aus Athan. Kircher's Musurgia universalis) 26
XVI.—XVII. **Merula** (Tarquinio) Canzon a tre. (Nach der zweiten Ausg. 1639) 29, 31
XVIII. **Neri** (Massimiliano) Canzone del terzo tuono (1644) 32
XIX. **Neri** (Massimiliano) Sonata (1651) 34
XX. **Neri** (Massimiliano) Bruchstücke aus einer Sonate für 3 Flöten, 2 Violinen, Violetta und Tiorba o Viola (1651) 38
XXI. **Marini** (Biagio) Sonate für 2 Violinen und Bass (1655) . . . 39
XXII. **Marini** (Biagio) Sonate für Violine und Bass (1655) 40
XXIII. **Legrenzi** (Giovanni) Sonate für 2 Violinen und Bass (1655) . 42

No.

XXIV. **Legrenzi** (Giovanni) Sonate für 2 Violinen, Viola alta, Viola Tenore und Viola da brazzo (1663) 43
XXV. **Vitali** (Giov. Batt.) Balletto a tre [Due Violini col suo Basso continuo] (Aus Op. I, 1666) 46
XXVI. **Vitali** (Giov. Batt.) Sonata a due Violini col suo Basso continuo per l'Organo (Op. 2, 1667) 47
XXVII. **Vitali** (Giov. Batt.) Sonata a due Violini e Organo (Aus Op. 5, 1669) 48
XXVIII. **Vitali** (Giov. Batt.) Capriccio a 4, due Violini, Alto e Violone (1669) 49
XXIX. **Uccellini** (Marco) Zwei Stücke aus den „Sinfonie Boscarecie" a Violino Solo e Basso (1669) 51
XXX. **Legrenzi** (Giov.) Sonate für 2 Violinen und Bass (1671) . . 52
XXXI. **Mazzaferrata** (Giov. Batt.) Sonate für 2 Violinen und Bass (1674) 53
XXXII. **Bassani** (Giov. B.) Balletto Corrente, Giga und Sarabanda für 2 Violinen und Bass (1677) 56
XXXIII. **Bassani** (Giov. B.) Sonate für 2 Violinen, Violoncello (ad libitum) und Orgel (1683) 58
XXXIV. **Bassani** (Giov. B.) Sonate für 2 Violinen und Bass (1683) . . 62
XXXV. **Torelli** (G.) Sonate für Violino solo, Violoncello obligato und Cembalo. (Gegen Ende des 17. Jahrh.) 64
XXXVI. **Torelli** (Giuseppe) Concerto con due Violini che concertano soli. (Aus Op. VIII, 1709) 68
XXXVII. **Veracini** (Antonio) Sonata a tre (1692) 76
XXXVIII. **Veracini** (Antonio) Sonata da Camera für Violine und Violone oder Arciluto und Cimbalo (Op. 3, 1696) 78

Alphabetisches Verzeichnis.

Allegri 26
Banchieri 10, 12
Bassani 56, 58, 62
Farina 19
Fontana 21, 23
Gabrieli 4, 7, 13, 15
Legrenzi 42, 43, 52
Marini 17, 18, 39, 40
Maschera 1, 2

Mazzaferrata 53
Merula 29, 31
Mont' Albano 25
Neri 32, 34, 38
Torelli 64, 68
Uccellini 51
Veracini 76, 78
Vitali 46, 47, 48, 49

Nᵒ I. Canzon da sonare à 4 von Florentio Maschera.
(K. Bibliothek zu Brüssel)

1.

La Capriola, Canzon.

(Nach der zweiten Auflage) 1593.

Canto.

Alto.

Tenore.

Basso.

№ II. Canzon da sonare à 4 von Flor. Maschera.
(K. Bibliothek zu Brüssel)

(Nach der zweiten Ausgabe) 1593.

Nº III. Canzon per sonar. Primi toni.
(K. Bibliothek zu Berlin)

Giov. Gabrieli 1597.

6.

Nᵒ IV. Sonata pian e forte. Alla quarta bassa.
(K. Bibliothek zu Berlin.)

Giov. Gabrieli 1597.

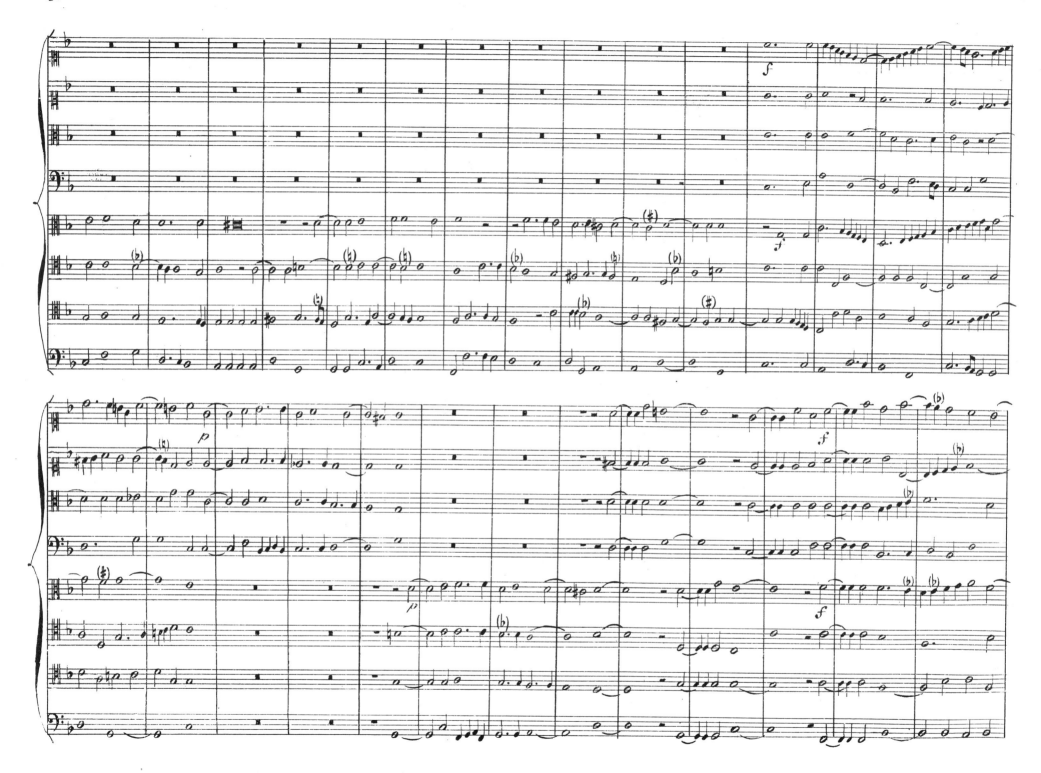

Nᵒ V. Fantasia in Eco movendo un Registro, von Adriano Banchieri.

(Nach der zweiten Ausgabe) 1603.

Canto

Alto.

Tenore.

Basso.

No. VI. Fantasia von Adriano Banchieri
(K. Bibliothek zu Brüssel)

(Nach der zweiten Ausgabe) 1603.

Nᵒ VII. Sonata con tre Violini
(K. Bibliothek zu Berlin)

Giov. Gabrieli. 1615.

Basso se piace.

№ VIII. Canzon à 6 von Giov. Gabrieli
(K. Bibliothek zu Berlin.)

1615.

Violini.

Cornetto.

Tenore.

Trombon.

Basso Trombon.

№ IX. *La Martinenga Corente a 3.*
(*Bibliothek des Liceo mus. zu Bologna.*)

Aus Opus 3 von Biagio Marini. 1622.

Il Priulino. Balletto & Corente.

No X. Romanesca per Violino Solo e Basso se piace

Von Biagio Marini, 1620, dedicirt:
Al Signor Gioan Battista Magni
Giouanetto di aspettatione nel Violino.

Seconda Parte

Corente.

N° XI. *Bruchstücke aus dem „Canto" des „Capriccio stravagante" v. Carlo Farina.* ✱
(*K. Bibliothek zu Dresden.*)
1627.

Il Pifferino.

Lira Variata.

Qui fornisce la Lira Variata.

Qui fornisce il Pifferino.

Qui si bate con il legno del archetto sopra le corde.

✱ *Bei den Doppelgriffen und Accorden ist die zweite u. dritte Stimme in dem von mir benützten Exemplare mit Dinte, wahrscheinlich von der Hand des Componisten hinzugefügt. Ich gebe den Satz so, wie er in dem auf der Dresdner Bibliothek befindlichen Originaldrucke, inclusive der hier hinzugeschriebenen Noten vorliegt.*

20.

Nº XII. Sonata à tre von Giov. Battista Fontana.
(Bibliothek des Liceo mus. zu Bologna.)

Sonata à doi Violini

gegen 1630.

Trillo espreßo in note.

Nᵒ XIII. Sonata a Violino Solo v. Battista Fontana
(Bibliothek des Liceo mus zu Bologna.)

gegen 1630.

N.º XIV. Sinfonia a duoi Violini e Basso v. Mont'Albano.
(Bibliothek des Liceo mus. zu Bologna.)

Castelletti.

1629.

No. XV. Symphonia
à 4. Duoi Violini, Alto, & Basso di Viola.

Gregorio Allegri. Vor 1650.
aus Anath. Kircher's Musurgia universalis.

Canzon detta la Cancelliera.

N.o XVI. Canzon à trè von Tarquinio Merula.
(Bibliothek des Liceo mus. zu Bologna)

Nach der zweiten Ausgabe 1639.

Violini

Basso.

Organo.

No. XVII. Canzon à tre von Tarquinio Merula.
(Bibliothek des Liceo mus. zu Bologna.)

Canzon detta la Visconta.

(Nach der zweiten Ausgabe) 1639.

Nᵒ XVIII Canzone del terzo tuono.
(K. Bibliothek zu Berlin)

Massimiliano Neri. 1644.

№ XIX.
(K. Bibliothek zu Berlin.)

Massimiliano Neri 1651.

Sonata.

Violini

Viola

Basso.

Nº XX. *Bruchstücke aus einer Sonate für 3 Flöten, 2 Violinen, Violetta u Tiorba o Viola.*
(*K.Bibliothek zu Berlin*)

Massimiliano Neri. 1651.

№ XXI. Sonate für 2 Violinen und Baß.
(Bibliothek des Liceo mus. zu Bologna)

Dolcemente.

Biagio Marini (1655.)

Violini

Basso.

Allegro.

Nº XXII. Sonate für Violine und Bass.
(Bibliothek des Liceo mus. zu Bologna.)

Biagio Marini. (1655.)

Terza parte.

N° XXIII. *Sonate für 2 Violinen und Bass.*
(K. Bibliothek zu Berlin.)

La Cornara. Allegro

Giovanni Legrenzi 1655.

N.º XXIV Sonate für 2 Violinen, Viola alto, Viola Tenore u. Viola da brazzo.

(K. Bibliothek zu Berlin)

Giovanni Legrenzi 1663.

Sonata a 5. La Fugazza

N.XXV. Balletto a tre, Due Violini col suo Basso continuo.
(Bibliothek des Liceo mus. zu Bologna.)

Aus Op. I. von Giov. Batt. Vitali. (1666.)

Corrente.

Grave

N.° XXVI *Sonata a due Violini col suo Basso continuo per l'Organo.*
(*Bibliothek des Liceo mus. zu Bologna.*)

Giov. Batt. Vitali Op. 2. (1667.)

N.º XXVII. *Sonata a due Violini e Organo.*
(Bibliothek des Liceo mus. zu Bologna.)

Aus Op. 5 von Giov. Batt. Vitali (1669)

Sonata. La Graziani.

Vivace.

Violini

Organo.

Vivace.

No. XXXVIII. Capriccio a 4, due Violini, Alto e Violone.
(Bibliothek des Liceo mus. zu Bologna.)

Giov. Batt. Vitali. 1669.

No. XXIX. *Zwei Stücke aus den "Sinfonie Boscarecie" à Violino Solo e Basso.*
(K. Bibliothek zu Brüssel.)

Symphonia. La Suavissima.

Marco Uccellini. 1669.

No XXX. Sonate für 2 Violinen und Bass.
(Bibliothek des Liceo mus zu Bologna.)

Giov. Legrenzi 1671.

La Rosetta.

№ XXXI. Sonate für 2 Violinen und Bass.
(Bibliothek des Liceo mus. zu Bologna.)

Mazzaferrata. 1674.

(Allegro.)

Violini

Basso.

Continuo.

No. XXXII. Balletto Corrente, Giga und Sarabanda für 2 Violinen u. Bass.
(Bibliothek des Liceo mus. zu Bologna.)

Balletto. Largo.

Giov. B. Bassani. 1677.

Corrente. Allegro.

Giga.

Sarabanda. Presto.

No. XXIII. Sonate für 2 Violinen, Violoncello (ad libitum) und Orgel.
(Bibliothek des Liceo mus. zu Bologna.)

Giov. B. Bassani. 1683.

Allegro.

Violini

Violoncello à benplacito

Organo.

No. XXXIV Sonate für 2 Violinen und Bass.
(Bibliothek des Liceo mus. zu Bologna.)

Giov. B. Bassani. 1683.

Grave.

Presto

Die Orgelstimme geht durchaus im unisono mit der Bassstimme, ausgenommen einige Stellen, bei denen dies bemerkt ist.

Basso.

Org.

Grave.

Basso.

Org.

No. XXXV. Sonate für Violino Solo, Violoncello obligato u. Cembalo.
(K. Privat-Musiksammlung zu Dresden.)

G. Torelli (gegen Ende des 17. Jahrh.)

N° XXXVI. Concerto con due Violini che concertano soli.

Aus Op. VIII. v. Giuseppe Torelli. 1708.

No. XXXVII. Sonata à tre.

(Bibliothek des Liceo mus. zu Bologna.)

Antonio Veracini. 1692. Op. 1.

No XXXVIII. Sonata da Camera für Violine und Violone oder Arciluto und Cimbalo.
(Bibliothek des Liceo mus. zu Bologna)

Ant. Veracini. Op.3. 1696.

80.

Vivace.

Violone e Cimb. unis.